Sixth Grade Science Experiments

By Thomas Bell

Home School Brew Press
www.HomeSchoolBrew.com

Cove Image © amplion - Fotolia.com

Table of Contents

Disclaimer

This book was developed for parents and students of no particular state; while it is based on common core standards, it is always best to check with your state board to see what will be included on testing.

About Us

Homeschool Brew was started for one simple reason: to make affordable Homeschooling books! When we began looking into homeschooling our own children, we were astonished at the cost of curriculum. Nobody ever said homeschool was easy, but we didn't know that the cost to get materials would leave us broke.

We began partnering with educators and parents to start producing the same kind of quality content that you expect in expensive books...but at a price anyone can afford.

We are still in our infancy stages, but we will be adding more books every month. We value your feedback, so if you have any comments about what you like or how we can do better, then please let us know!

To add your name to our mailing list, go here: http://www.homeschoolbrew.com/mailing-list.html

The Scientific Process: Activities and Experiments

1.Observing and recording

What you need:

- Pencil
- Paper
- Ruler
- A scale
- An object from your room

What you do:

- Take the object and lay it on the table.
- Using your pencil and paper, draw the object as best you can. If the object has straight edges, use a ruler.
- Measure the dimensions of the object, and label the drawing appropriately.
- Write down additional characteristics of the object, such as the color, texture, and weight.

What you should learn:

- This exercise should teach you how to properly observe something, as well as record data in a scientific way.

Question:

- In what phase of the scientific process do you normally observe and record?

2. Writing materials and methods

What you need:
- Pencil
- Paper
- All the materials that you choose to include for the method you write
- A friend, teacher, or parent

What you do:
- Write a materials and methods guide for making a peanut butter and jelly sandwich.
- Include all details needed, as if the person reading your materials and methods has no idea about sandwich making.
- Give the materials and methods to the other person.
- The second person should follow the methods EXACTLY, using ONLY things that are on the materials list.

What you should learn:
- This should show you how important it is to be precise and detailed when writing materials and methods.

Questions:
- Did everything go according to plan?
- Was everything you need on the materials list?

- Is there any possibility that your methods could have accidentally been interpreted in the wrong way?

3. Forming your hypothesis
- Pencil
- Paper
- Empty plastic water bottle
- Full plastic water bottle
- Wine cork
- Penny
- Pencil
- Paperclip
- Anything else you would like to test that can go in water

What you do:
- Hypothesize, for each object, whether it will float or sink.
- Fill a bucket or bathtub with water.
- Check whether each object floats or sinks
- Record your data

What you should learn:
- How to try to form a hypothesis

Question:
- How accurate were your hypotheses?

4. Identifying variables
What you need:
- Pencil
- Paper

- Bouncy ball
- Measuring tape

What you do:
- Take the ball to different locations and drop it from the same height.
- Measure how high the ball bounces on different surfaces.
- Measure the height of the bouncing and record your data.
- Identify in your results which variable is your independent variable, which is your dependent variable, and what your controlled variables are.

What you should learn:
- How to identify which variables are which, and how important it is to control them.

Questions:
- What is your independent variable?
- What is your dependent variable?
- What are your control variables?

5. Drawing graphs

What you need:
- Pencil
- Paper
- Ruler

What you do:
- Go around the house or room and count how many objects you see that are green and record your data

- Go around the house or room and count how many objects you see that are red and record your data
- Go around the house or room and count how many objects you see that are yellow and record your data
- Repeat for as many colors as you like
- After you have counted your objects and recorded your data, carefully draw a bar graph with a ruler that shows your results. Make sure to label your axes properly.
- Calculate how many objects you counted on average per color

What you should learn:

- How to draw a graph, and how to process your data

Questions

- How does looking at a graph change your perception of your data?
- Is a graph useful for interpretation of the data?
- How many objects did you count on average?

Properties of Matter: Activities and Experiments

1. Making naked eggs

What you need:

- Eggs
- Transparent vinegar
- Large container
- Spoon
- Pencil and lab book

What you do:

- Put several eggs in the container
- Cover the eggs with vinegar completely, and notice how small bubbles begin to form.
- Put the eggs on the bench and leave them overnight
- The next day carefully and gently take the eggs out with a spoon and feel them.
- Record your observations.

What you should learn:

- The eggs become soft because the vinegar is an acid, called acetic acid. The acid reacts with the calcium carbonate in the shell, which causes small carbon dioxide bubbles to form. The carbon floats away in the bubbles, leaving a soft egg behind.

Question:
- Is this a physical change or a chemical change?

2. Making Sugar crystals

What you need:
- Sugar
- Stove
- Water
- String
- Scissor
- Button
- Pencil
- Pot
- Spoon
- Glass
- Lab book

What you do:
- Boil some water in the pot on the stove.
- Once it is boiling turn off the stove.
- Put sugar in the water spoon by spoon.
- Continue adding sugar until no more sugar can be dissolve.
- Let the water cool.
- In the meantime, tie a string that is the same height as the glass to a pencil in the middle.
- Tie a button to the other end of the string.

- Place the pencil across the top of the glass, letting the button fall to the bottom.
- Fill the glass with the now cold sugar water solution.
- Put the glass in a warm place and leave it undisturbed for a few days, checking on it from time to time.
- When the water has fully evaporated, you can see the sugar crystals hanging on the string. You can even eat these sugar crystals!

What you should learn:
- Students should grasp the concepts of solutions and evaporation.

Question:
- Where did the water go?
- How did the sugar crystals taste?

3. Baking soda and vinegar reaction

What you need:
- Baking soda (not baking powder)
- Transparent vinegar
- Glass
- Pencil and lab book

What you do:
- Put the glass in the sink, since you will make a mess
- Pour some of the baking powder in the bottom of the glass
- Pour some of the vinegar into the glass

- Record your observations

What you should learn:
- Vinegar, as you learned in a previous experiment, is a kind of acid called acetic acid. Baking soda is sodium bicarbonate, which is a base. The acid reacts with the base, causing a chemical reaction. Together they form carbonic acid, which is very unstable. It breaks apart into water and carbon dioxide, which is what you see happening in the glass.

Question:
- Is this a physical change or a chemical change?

4. Air pressure can crush

What you need:
- An empty and washed soda can
- Stove
- Cooking tongs
- Cold water
- Bowl

What you do:
- Fill the bowl with cold water. The colder the water is the better it will be for the experiment.
- Add a full tablespoon of water to the contents of the can.
- Place the can on the stove and turn it on

- Once the water starts bubbling and you see some vapor rising from the can, then you know the water is evaporating. Wait 1 more minute.
- This step is the important step. After the can has been sitting for 1 more minute, use the tongs to grab the can. Quickly flip the can over and plunge it top-down into the cold water. It is important to not hesitate when you carry out this step.
- Record your observations

What you should learn:
- Before you heated the can, it was filled with water and air. When you turned on the stove to boil the water, it changed from a liquid to a gas. When water is in a gas state, the molecules are much further apart from one another, and it takes up more space. Because of this the water vapor pushes some of the air out of the can. When you flip the can over and put it in the water, it returns to its liquid state, and takes up less space. Because it takes up less space, there is now less pressure inside the can, and the pressure outside the can is great enough to crush the can.

Question:
- Is this a chemical change or a physical change?

5. Magic Milk

What you need:
- A bowl
- Milk
- Liquid dish detergent
- Various shades of food coloring
- Pencil and lab book

What you do:
- Pour milk into the bowl
- Add several drops of food coloring to the center of the bowl, all in the same spot.
- Repeat for several different colors.
- Carefully drop a single drop of detergent into the center of the milk where the colored spot is.
- Record your observations.

What you should learn:
- Milk is mostly just made of water, but it also contains protein and fat. The important component in this experiment, however, is the soap. Dish soap molecules have 2 very differently behaving ends. One end of the molecule wants to dissolves in water. The other end does not like water and is repelled away from it; instead, it wants to grab onto fat molecules. For this reason, the soap moves throughout the plate, grabbing onto loose fat molecules. Because of this, the food coloring in the milk is pushed all around. Without the food coloring this

would still occur, but you would not be able to see it.

Question:

- What will happen if you add more dish soap after the first drop? Try it in different areas of the bowl and find out for yourself!

The Human Body: Activities and Experiments

1. Heart rate investigations

What you need:
- A watch with a seconds hand
- A pencil
- Paper

What you do:
- Sit in a relaxed place, and try not to do anything strenuous for a few minutes. Just breathe normally and try to relax.
- Using your first two fingers, feel your neck, just to the side of your windpipe. Search around with your fingers until you find your pulse.
- Look at your watch and count the how many times your heart beats in a ten second period.
- Multiply this number by 6, and now you have the number of beats per minute.
- Record your result
- Now, find an area to safely run around, and run for 5 minutes. Work hard so that you get tired.

- Repeat the process of counting and multiplying your heartbeats.
- Record your data.

What you should learn:
- When you check your pulse in this area what you can feel is your carotid artery. The pulse indicates the beating of your heart, which is important for carrying blood around the body. When you exercise, your body needs more oxygen, which means your body needs more blood circulation. Your heart compensates for this by pumping harder and faster.

Question:
- Why does your body need more oxygen when you exercise? To answer this question, you might need to do some research with a computer.

2. Investigating your bladder capacity

What you need:
- A large measuring cup
- Paper
- Pencil and lab book

What you do:
- Wait until you feel the need to urinate.
- Go to the bathroom and carefully collect your urine in the measuring cup.
- Record how much urine you released.
- Pour your urine in the toilet and rinse the measuring cup.

- Repeat the process several times, always waiting until you need to go, and always recording your data.
- Average all of your data.

What you should learn:

- Everyone will have a different average urine capacity. This is due to the size of the bladder. Females will have a lower bladder capacity on average, since they have smaller bladders. This is because they also need space in their abdomens for the uterus, which men do not have.

Questions:

- Does your pee gross you out? Don't worry! It may smell bad, but it's completely sterile!

3. Measuring lung capacity

What you need:

- Large empty plastic bottle
- Large and deep bowl
- Water
- Measuring cup
- 30 cm flexible plastic tubing, such as aquarium tubing
- Marker
- Pencil and lab book

What you do:

- Using the measuring cup, measure out 100 ml of water. Pour the 100 ml into the bottle
- Using the marker, label the water level of the bottle.
- Add 100 ml more, and mark the new level as well.
- Repeat until the whole bottle is marked.
- Put water in the large and deep bowl, until there is a good layer of about 10 cm covering the bottom.
- Fill the bottle with water until it is completely full.
- Cover the opening of the bottle with you hand so that no water can get out, and flip it upside down with the top in the bowl. Make sure not to remove your fingers until the mouth of the bottle is completely in the water.
- Without letting any air into it, insert one end of the plastic tubing into the bottle.
- Inhale deeply, and exhale all the air into the tube.
- Measure how much air is in the bottle and calculate your lung capacity.
- Record your data.

What you should learn:
- Lung capacity is usually measured with a tool called a spirometer, but in this do-it-yourself setup, we can easily measure our

lung capacity. We use displacement in this experiment. This means that we displace the water in the bottle with the air from our lungs. This lets us see exactly how much we exhaled in ml, since we marked the bottle.

Questions:
- Compare your results with those of an adult and a friend. Is your lung capacity larger or smaller than theirs?
- Why do you think this is?

4. Depth perception test

What you need
- 2 pencils and lab book

What you do:
- Hold the two pencils sideways and at arms length, with the erasers facing inwards
- Close one eye and bring the two pencils closer together in front of you.
- Try to touch the eraser tips together. If you miss, extend your hands to the side and try again.
- Repeat this 5 times, and record how many times you successfully touched the eraser tips together.
- Repeat the experiment, but this time with both of your eyes open.
- Record the data.

What you should learn:

- It is much easier to touch the ends of the pencils together when both of your eyes are open. This is because of depth perception. Two eyes are better than one because they work together as a team. Because the two eyes will see things from different angles depending on the object's distance from the eyes, the brain can use this information and determine how far away the object is.

Question:
- When is depth perception important to have?
- Are there any other factors you can think of that help with depth perception? Hint: look at things that are far away, and try to ask yourself the following question: How do I know it is far away?

5. Reaction time test

What you need:
- A ruler
- A partner
- Pencil and lab book

What you do:
- Have your partner hold the ruler at the end, near the largest number
- Your partner should then let the ruler hang down
- Put your hand at the bottom of the ruler, but do not touch it. Get ready to grab it.

- The partner should then drop the ruler after a random interval of time. This is important because you should not be able to guess when the ruler will drop.
- When the ruler is dropped you should catch it between your thumb and forefinger.
- Record the markings at which your fingers grabbed the ruler.
- Repeat 5 times and make an average of the distance the ruler fell.

What you should learn:

- When you do this task your body is doing many things at once. First, your eyes will receive visual information about the ruler dropping. Then, your eyes will send this information to the brain, which will process the information and send signals to the muscles. Your muscles will then contract and move your body, allowing you to catch the ruler.

Question:

- Using the distance that the ruler fell, calculate how long your reaction time was. For this you can use the following formula:

- $$t = \sqrt{\frac{2y}{g}}$$

- In this formula, t is time, y is the distance in cm that the ruler fell, and g is 980 cm/sec^2, due to gravity. Get a teacher or parent to check your work.

Earth / Moon / Sun: Activities and Experiments

1. Calculate how long it would take you to reach the moon

What you need:

- Pencil
- Paper
- Calculator

What you do:

- Consider the following pieces of information: You are travelling down the highway at 70 miles per hour.
- Imagine the highway could take you all the way to the moon. How long do you think it will take you to get there at this speed? Guess, and record your guess.
- How long will it take you to travel 70 miles at this speed?
- Now calculate how long will it take you to travel 100 miles. If you need help, ask a parent or teacher.
- Now consider how far away the moon is: 238,900 miles!
- Calculate how many hours it will take you to travel to the moon at this speed.

- Calculate how many days this is.

What you learn:
- The moon is far away, and now you should have an idea of how far away it really is. You may also have learned some more about how to calculate speeds and distances.

Questions:
- How long would it take?
- How close was your guess?
- Does it take more or less time than you expected?

2. Calculate how long it would take you to reach the sun

What you need:
- Pencil
- Paper
- Calculator

What you do:
- Just as in the previous experiment, we are going to calculate how long it will take to reach a certain distance
- Imagine we are still going 70 mph, but this time the highway stretches all the way to the surface of the sun!
- Again, guess how long it would take, and record your answer.
- Now consider that the sun is very far away. It is 92,960,000 miles away!

- How many hours would it take you to get to the sun from earth?
- How many days does this equal?
- How many years does this equal?

What you should learn:

- The sun is very, very far away! At this speed, you would not even make it there in your lifetime. This shows just how far away it really is.

Questions:

- How long would it take?
- How close was your guess?

3. Calculate how long it takes light to reach the earth from the sun

What you need:

- Pencil
- Paper
- Calculator

What you do:

- First, guess how long it takes for light to travel from the sun to the earth.
- Record your guess
- Then, use the following information to calculate the proper answer.
- As previously mentioned, the sun is 92,960,000 miles away.
- Light travels very fast. It goes 670,616,629 miles per hour!
- How many hours does it take for light from the sun to reach the earth?

- Calculate how many minutes this is.

What you should learn:

- Although the sun is very far away from the earth, light travels very quickly. That's why it takes just a matter of minutes for light to reach us here on earth.

Questions:

- How long did you calculate would it take?
- How close was your guess?

4. Making a sundial

What you need:

- A paper plate
- Markers
- A straw
- Ruler
- Pins
- Pencil and lab book
- Sticky tack

What you do:

- Start this activity on a sunny day, at around 11 am.
- Turn the paper plate onto its back.
- Use a ruler to find the center of the paper plate, and poke a hole through the center with the pencil.
- Use the markers to draw the numbers 1-12 on the plate, just like they are on a

clock. Draw the numbers 12, 3, 6, and 9 first, to make it easier.

- Just before 12 o'clock, go outside and take the plate, pins, and straw with you. Put the plate in a sunny place on the ground, and put the straw inside push the straw down through the hole. Keep the straw facing up, and keep it as straight as possible. You can use sticky tack to keep the straw in place if need be.
- Now, at exactly 12, take the plate and rotate it so that the shadow of the straw points towards 12.
- Pin the plate in place to the ground, on a flat surface. Do not allow the plate to move.
- Come back in 1 hour and look at the clock. Record the location of the shadow and the number it points to.

What you should learn:
- You can use the position of the sun to determine the time. This is an old technique that has been used for a long time. This works because of the sun's shifting position in the sky during the earth's rotation.

5. Simulating the phases of the moon.

What you need:
- Small flashlight

- Shoebox with a lid
- Scissors
- Black thread
- Transparent tape
- White polystyrene ball, about the size of a golf ball
- Black paint
- Paint brush
- Black paper
- Pencil and lab book

What you do:
- Paint the inside of the box and the inside of the lid with black paint and let it dry.
- Cut 8 holes in the box, 3 on each long side, and 1 on each short side, as in the picture below. You can use a hole punch to make this easier, if you have one. Also cut a larger hole for your flashlight, as illustrated.

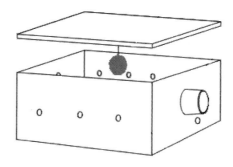

- Next, hang the polystyrene ball from the lid of the box, using the black thread and the tape.
- Tape a small flap of black paper over each hole.
- Shine the flashlight through the large hole, and look through each small hole, 1 at a time.
- Record your observations in the form of descriptions and drawings.

What you should learn:

- When you look through the small holes in the box, this is like a simulation of the phases of the moon. Looking through each hole is like seeing the moon from a different angle, as we do during the different times of the month. The flashlight represents the sun.

Questions:

- What are the names of the different phases of the moon? Can you correlate those phases with the different angles you see through your box?

Characteristics of Plants: Activities and Experiments

1. Coloring flowers

What you need:

- 5 glasses or plastic cups.
- 5 different food coloring colors
- 7 or 8 white freshly cut daises
- Pencil and lab book

What you do:

- Fill the glasses half way with lukewarm water.
- Add 20- 30 drops of food coloring, until the color is nice and visible in the water.
- Put a daisy in each glass.
- Return in 1 hour to observe and record your results. Come back every hour and record your results again. Sometimes the process will take up to a whole day, and sometimes it will be very fast.

What you should learn:

- The daisies become colored because the stem sucks up the colored water. Usually roots of the plant deliver the water to the stems, but water can be taken up by stems alone.

Questions:

- What is the name of the structure that sucks up the water?
- What do you think will happen if you slit the stem up the middle and put each half into a different colored solution? Give it a try with your last couple of flowers!

2. Make pressed flower specimens

What you need:

- 5 freshly picked flowers. Go outside and find your favorite types and colors!
- White sheets of paper
- Some heavy books
- Pencil and lab book
- White paper

What you do:

- Line the inside of a heavy books pages with sheets of white paper
- Lay the flowers, one in between each page.
- Close the book and lay many heavy books on top
- Leave the books undisturbed for at least 3 weeks. The longer you leave them the better they will be pressed.
- Identify each species in your lab book and paste the samples inside, labeling and describing each plant type. You might

need the help of a parent, teacher, or the Internet to find it all out.

What you should learn:

- You may have had to do a bit of research to find out which plants were the ones you picked flowers from. You learned how to collect and document botanical samples as well.

Questions:

- What is the function of a flower?
- Why do flowers have interesting appearances and smells?

3. Investigating gravitropism

What you need:

- Shoe box with lid
- Small square flower pot with young radish plant

What you do:

- Put the plant inside the shoebox on its side.
- Close the box and leave it on the bench for 24 hours.
- Open the box and observe/ record the results.

What you should learn:

- Since radish plants grow quickly it should be possible for you to see the change in direction of growth after 24 hours. This is due to gravitropism, where the plants tend to grow against the force of gravity.

Questions:

- Why do we put the plant in the shoebox? If you don't know the answer, try to answer it again after the next experiment. If it is still hard to answer you should review the different types of variables in chapter 1.

4. Investigating phototropism

- Taller cardboard box.
- Small flower pot with young radish plant
- Pencil and lab book
- Scissors
- Adjustable table lamp
- Camera (optional)

What you do:

- Cut a hole in the side of the box.
- Put the plant inside the box.
- Adjust the table lamp so that it shines in the hole in the side of the box.
- Record your observations every 24 hours for a few days, taking pictures if possible, for your lab book.

What you should learn:

- Plants do not only display the ability to grow against gravity, but they also have the ability to grow towards the light. This is called phototropism.

Question:

- Why is it better to use the box with a hole, instead of just the table lamp, next to the plant? Do you think the plant grow differently? Try it if you like!

5. Investigating effects of fertilizers

What you need:
- 3 pots
- Bag of soil; enough for 3 pots
- Seeds of your choice, all from the same plant.
- Organic fertilizer
- Chemical fertilizer
- Ruler
- Pencil and Lab book
- Water

What you do:
- Fill pots with soil and plant 3 seeds.
- Keep all three pots in the same conditions, and water them at the same time and with the same amount of water.
- Following instructions on the container or bag, use the organic fertilizer for 1 plant, chemical fertilizer for another plant, and no fertilizer for the third plant.
  Measure the growth of the plants every day for 2 weeks.
- Observe and record the results.

What you should learn:

- Different types of fertilizer will affect each plant slightly differently, so in this case we cannot generalize. This just allows you to design a small experiment, see the effects of different fertilizers, and try to interpret the results.

Questions:
- Which fertilizer worked better for your plant?
- Were there any problems with the growth of the plants? If so, why do you think this may be?
- What is your dependent variable?
- What is your independent variable?
- What are your control variables?

Energy, Force, & Motion: Activities and Experiments

1. Investigating kinetic and potential energy

What you need:

- Thin wooden board
- Wooden block, or a small stack of books
- Toy skateboard
- 3 metal washers
- Rubber band
- Ruler/ meter stick
- Pencil and lab book

What you do:

- Build a small ramp on a smooth surface using the thin wooden board and the block.
- Hold the skateboard at the top of the ramp and let go.
- Allow skateboard to roll down and off the ramp without interrupting it.
- Measure the distance from the starting point.
- Record your results.
- Attach a washer to the skateboard using the rubber band.

- Repeat the measurement with these conditions.
- Record your data.
- Add another washer and repeat.
- Record your data.
- Add the third washer and repeat.
- Record your data.

What you should learn:
- When the skateboard has the washers attached to it, it has more mass. This gives it more potential energy when it sits at the top of the ramp. When you push it down, this potential energy is transferred to kinetic energy. The greater the potential energy, the greater the kinetic energy. That is why the skateboard travels further with the washers attached.

Question:
- Can you think of any other examples of potential energy being converted to kinetic energy?

2. Observing Newton's third law in action
What you need:
- Balloons
- Paper and pencil

What you do:
- This experiment is easy!
- You start by blowing up the balloon, but not tying it.
- Hold the opening downward and let go.

- Repeat several times and record your observations.
- Describe what is happening in terms of the third law of motion.
- To make this one more fun, you can also create a small tube of paper that you tape to the balloon. Then, string a long string through this tube. Tie one end of the string at one end of the room, and one at the other. Then repeat this experiment and see how the balloon flies down your newly created balloon highway!

What you should learn:
- This should give students the chance to revise and refresh their memory of newton's third law. It also gives students a chance to explain a physical phenomenon in terms of a scientific description.

Question:
- What is Newton's third law and what does it mean?

3. Observing Newton's first law in action
What you need:
- Full 2 liter plastic bottle
- Wax paper
- Kitchen table
- Pencil and lab book

What you do:

- Place the wax paper at the edge of the table, with some hanging off the edge.
- Place the full bottle on the paper.
- Quickly and sharply pull the wax paper out from underneath the bottle.
- Record your observations.

What you should learn:
- If you managed to do this properly, the paper should have been removable without tipping the bottle over. This is due to the effect seen in Newton's first law. Because of the heavy bottle's inertia, it did not fall.

Questions:
- What forces were acting on the bottle?
- What forces were acting on the wax paper?
- What would happen if the bottle were much lighter? Why?

4. Friction studies
What you need:
- Board
- Wax paper
- Foil
- Block or stack of books
- Pencil and lab book
- Tape
- Toy skateboard
- Ruler or meter stick

What you do:
- As you did previously in experiment 1, set up the board with the block to make a ramp. Do this on a smooth surface.
- As you performed in experiment 1, allow the skateboard to race down the surface, and measure the distance it traveled.
- Record your data.
- Using tape, attach the wax paper to the board.
- Repeat the measurement and record your results
- Using tape, attach foil to the surface of the board.
- Repeat your measurements and record the results.

What you should learn:
- Friction is one of the variables that determine the movement of an object through space. Different amounts of friction are introduced in this experiment through the different surface materials of the ramp. This shows you that surface that generate less friction allow the skateboard to travel further than the surfaces that generate more friction.

Question:
- What would happen if there was no friction at all?

5. Making a potato powered clock

What you need:
- 2 potatoes
- 2 small pieces of copper wire
- 2 galvanized nails (it is important that they are galvanized)
- 3 clip wire units (clips connected to each other with a wire in between)
- 1 low-voltage clock (uses 1-2 Volt battery)
- Pencil and lab book

What you do:
- Remove the battery from the clock
- Insert the galvanized nails into the potatoes, 1 in each.
- Insert the small lengths of copper wire into the potatoes, 1 in each, at as far a distance from the galvanized nail as possible.
- Use one of the clips to attach the copper wire to the + terminal in the battery compartment.
- Use of the clips to attach the nail in the other potato to the – terminal in the battery compartment.
- Use the remaining clip to attach the remaining nail and copper wire in the adjacent potatoes.
- If everything worked your clock should be on now!
- See how long the potato battery lasts and record your result.

What you should learn:

- A potato in this scenario acts as an electrochemical cell. What this means is that chemical energy is being transferred to electric energy via the potato. The galvanized nails are covered in zinc, which is negatively charged. The copper is positively charged. When the nail comes into contact with a naturally occurring acid inside the potato, called phosphoric acid. This causes a chemical reaction that frees electrons. The copper takes up these electrons, and thus creates a circuit.

Question:
- Can you think of any other examples of one energy type being transferred into another energy type?

Electricity & Magnetism: Activities and Experiments

1. Making a compass

What you need:

- Sewing needle
- Cork
- Bar magnet
- Sticky tack
- Scissors or knife
- Bowl or dish of water
- Compass

What you do:

- Cut a circle of cork using the scissors or knife.
- Magnetize the needle by using 1 end of the bar magnet, and swiping the needle from one end to the other 50 times, always in the same direction. Rubbing in the other direction will demagnetize the sewing needle.
- Use the tack and stick the magnetized needle flat on the center of the cork.

- Put the cork in the water dish and wait for the needle to rotate to show which way is north.
- Check with your compass that this is correct.

What you should learn:

- When you use the magnet to magnetize the needle, it can interact with the magnetic field of the earth. Using cork allows the needle to float, and using water gives a mostly frictionless surface for the needle to rotate on. Over time the needle will lose the magnetic charge.

Question:

- How could this skill be useful?

2. Holding a charge

What you need:

- Paper straw
- Napkin

What you do:

- Do this experiment in a dry area
- Use the napkin and slide it up and down the straw, 20 or 30 times.
- Remove the napkin and put the straw in your open palm to see if it sticks.
- Record your results

What you should learn:

- When you rub the paper on the straw you electrically charge it, making the straw more negatively charged. When you bring it near your palm, it causes the palm to become positively charged, and they attract each other.

Question:

- Can you think of any other time when static electricity causes things to stick to you?

3. Eddy currents

What you need:

- A neodymium magnet
- A pencil and lab book
- 1 meter of copper, brass, or aluminum tubing, larger in diameter than the magnet
- 1 meter of non metallic tubing such as PVC pipe

What you do:

- Hold the metal pipe vertically, and drop your pencil through the pipe.
- Now, drop the magnet through the pipe.
- Try dropping the magnet and the pencil through the PVC pipe as well.
- Record your observations.

What you should learn:

- As the magnet is falling through the tube, the magnetic field around it is constantly changing, and the tube experiences this changing magnetic field. This causes something called eddy currents, which occur in the metal tubing. The eddy currents create a magnetic field that affects the course of the magnet's movement. The force inhibits the magnet's fall, causing it to move more slowly through the tube.

3. Shorting the circuit

What you need:

- 6 volt battery
- Length of copper wire with clips
- A strand of very thin iron wire. E.g. unbraided picture hanging wire

What you do:

- Attach one end of the clip to the battery
- Attach the other end of the clip to the thin iron wire
- Attach the other end of the iron wire to the other battery terminal.
- Slowly move the clip attached to the iron wire closer and closer to the battery along the iron wire.
- Observe what happens and record your results. (Caution: the wire will get very hot!)

What you should learn:

- If it worked properly the iron wire should have gotten hotter and hotter until it melts the wire and breaks the circuit. The thin iron wire has a higher resistance to electrical current compared to the copper wire. The voltage from the battery pushes electrons against the resistance, heating the wire. As you make the wire shorter by moving the clip closer to the battery, the wire gets hotter and hotter. Eventually this causes the wire to melt.

Question:

- How does this relate to the concept of a fuse? (Some research will be required to answer this question)

4. Insulators versus conductors

What you need:

- Several different small pieces of material e.g. wood, plastic, string, foil, etc.
- 6 volt battery
- 3 wire leads with clips
- 6 volt light bulb with leads
- Cutting board

What you do:

- Use the cutting board as the base for your circuit.
- Attach a wire to each terminal of the battery.
- Take the other end of the wire attached to the – end and attach it to one of the light bulb leads.
- Attach the third and yet unattached wire to the second light bulb lead.
- Now you should have 2 loose clips. When you attach them, if you made the circuit correctly, the light bulb should light up.

- Now, introduce your testing materials in between these two clips.
- Look at how this affects the brightness of the light, for each material.
- Observe and record the results.

What you should learn:

- If the material is an insulating material, the light will be more dim, or even completely off. The better the material conducts the brighter the light will shine.

Question:

- Which materials were good insulators?
- Which were good conductors?

5. Levitation with magnets

What you need:

- Paperclip
- A large strong magnet
- Thread
- Pencil and lab book
- Tape

What you do:

- Tape one end of the thread to the table.
- Tie the other end of the thread to the paperclip.
- Use the large magnet to attract the paperclip upward. Keep the magnet higher than the thread allows, suspending the paperclip in the air.

- Use a ruler to measure the distances at which the magnet still attracts the paperclip.

What you should learn:

- You should see how strong your magnet is! Magnets are amazing tools that can be used in all kinds of industrial applications. After seeing what you can do with a single magnet and paperclip, imagine what you could do with all the tools that engineers have available today.

Question:

- Can you think of another kind of technology that uses magnets?

Periodic Table: Activities and Experiments

1. Draw your own periodic table

What you need:
- Paper
- Pencil and colored pencils
- Pens
- Ruler

What you do:
- Draw your own periodic table
- Put it in your lab book

What you should learn:
- This should help you become more familiar with the periodic table, and now that you have your own that you drew yourself, you can proudly put it in your ever-filling lab book, or even put it on your wall!

Question:
- How many elements can you name from the top of your head?

2. Create an element information brochure

What you need:
- A computer
- A printer

- Paper

What you do:
- Choose an element from the periodic table
- Include such information as the name, how it got its name, the abbreviation, its atomic number, atomic mass, physical properties, chemical properties, abundance in the earth, places where it is found, what it can be used for, and anything else you can find out about it!
- Print your brochure and put it in your lab book.

What you should learn:
- You should have learned everything there is to know about your element!

Questions:
- Why did you choose the element you chose?
- Was it interesting to study that element? What other elements do you want to know more about?

3. Make a model of an atom

What you need:
- Arts and craft materials

What you do:
- Using whatever arts and crafts materials you like, create your own model of an atom.

- Your atom can be made in any way you like; it can be a 3 dimensional model, or a 2 dimensional model stuck onto cardboard. It can be suspended or sitting. It can be any way you like!
- Make sure that your model has something to represent electrons, protons, and neutrons.

What you should learn:
- This should reinforce your understanding of the atom, and provides a fun activity to transfer theoretical imaginary conceptions into tangible models!

Questions:
- How many electrons does your model atom have?
- Which element would it be?

4. Investigate the elemental composition of the human body

What you need:
- A computer with internet connection
- Pencil
- Lab book

What you do:
- Do some research to find out what kinds of elements are in the human body.
- Find out which elements we contain, and in what amounts.
- Record all of your findings in your lab book, and write down your sources.

What you should learn:
- Science is not always about doing experiments. A lot of the time, being a good scientist means searching for data. There have been so many scientists working on so many topics, finding something out can be as easy as searching with Google! In this activity you should learn what elements are contained within the human body, and maybe a little bit about why the distribution is this way.

Question:
- Which element is the most abundant in the human body?
- Is this abundance by weight, or by number of atoms?
- Is the answer going to be different if you change your criteria? If so, why?

5. Decorating your lab coat
What you need:
- Fresh white lab coat
- Many permanent markers

What you do:
- If you are going to be a scientist, you are going to need a lab coat one day! Now, you have the chance to design and decorate your (perhaps) very first lab coat!
- Using your permanent markers, design and draw a science themed lab coat. You

can include scientific symbols, elements, or anything related to science.

What you should learn:

- Designing and drawing your lab coat might just seem like a bit of fun, but keep in mind that safety in science is of the utmost importance. Since it is such an important and personal tool for scientists' safety, you want to like your lab coat, and enjoy wearing it.

Question:

- How do you think a lab coat helps with safety?

Photosynthesis: Activities and Experiments

1. Investigating the effect of sunlight deprivation

What you need:

- 2 inexpensive fast growing plants
- Water
- Light proof cupboard
- Ruler
- Pencil and lab book

What you do:

- Evaluate both plants in terms of color, height, and sturdiness. Does the plant look healthy?
- Record your observations.
- Place one plant on the windowsill and one plant in the cupboard.
- Over the period of 1 week, water the plants the same amount and at the same time, and make sure not to expose the plant in the dark to the light for too long.
- After 1 week, perform the same observations you did in the beginning.
- Record your results.

What you should learn:

- Sunlight is an integral part of a plant's growth and survival requirements. When you deprive them of it they cannot photosynthesize. This experiment shows you the drastic effect this can have on a plant's overall wellbeing.

Questions:
- What did the plant in the dark look like?
- How long did it take for these changes to occur?

2. Isolating chlorophyll

What you need:
- Handful of green plant leaves
- Cup
- Scissors
- Paper towel
- Oven
- Water
- Foil
- Test tubes with lids
- Mortar and pestle
- Acetone

What you do:
- Put the leaves in a cup.
- Pour boiling water over them, leave for 1 minute, then take out and dry them.
- Remove all veins from the leaves and throw them away, then cut the leaves up into small pieces.

- Put them on foil and put them in the oven for 20 min, at 40 degrees centigrade.
- Put the now dry leaves into a completely dry mortal and pestle and crush them.
- Put the crushed mixture into the test tube, and add 5-10 ml of acetone.
- Close the lid and shake, then wait 10 more minutes.
- Without shaking the it, return and look at the contents of the test tube.
- Observe and record any colors, layers of separation, and other characteristics of the mixture.

What you should learn:

- When you observe this mixture, you will see several things. The first think you may notice is that there seems to be a layer of greenish solution, under which there will be sediment of dark green powder. The chlorophyll, which is the green pigment responsible for absorbing the light, is now diluted in the acetone. The big pieces that you see are cellular debris, and smaller pieces may cause the solution to be foggy. If you would filter out the pieces, you should have an acetone solution with chlorophyll in it. In science, it is very common to have to separate different components of your samples with techniques similar to this.

Question:

- What would plants look like if there was no chlorophyll left in them?

3. Investigating oxygen release
What you need:
- Elodea- water plant
- Scissors
- Test tubes
- Water
- Baking soda
- Lamp
- Tape
- Clock or stopwatch
- Ruler
- Test tube rack or stand
- Pencil and lab book

What you do:
- Grab 1 sprig of your elodea plant.
- Tear off any leaves around the cut stem, and cut a small section of the stem again at an angle.
- Gently crush the cut end, and place the sprig cut-end-up in a test tube filled with water.
- Push it to the bottom.
- Place the lamp 5 cm from the test tube. Wait 1 minute
- Start your stopwatch and start counting bubbles. The bubbles will rise from the sprig, and your job is to count them for

the next 5 minutes. If no bubbles appear, recut and recrush the end of the stem.
- Record your results.
- Add a small amount of baking soda to the solution and repeat the process.
- After 1 minute, count and record the number of bubbles again.

What you should learn:
- This experiment can be a bit tricky, but if you managed to achieve it properly, you should have been able to count the number of bubbles that this plant released in a five-minute period. During the process of photosynthesis, oxygen is generated. The more oxygen is released, the more photosynthesis is occurring. When you add the baking soda, you are introducing more carbon dioxide to the plant, allowing faster photosynthesis rates.

Question:
- How many bubbles did the sprig release in a 5-minute period?
- Did the baking soda have the expected effect?

4. Making moss graffiti
What you need:
- A few handfuls of moss
- Non flavored yoghurt or buttermilk
- Beer

- Sugar
- Blender
- Paintbrush
- Container for moss paint
- Corn syrup

What you do:

- Wash the moss to remove as much dirt as possible.
- Add the moss, 2 cups of yoghurt or buttermilk, 2 cups of beer, and 1 teaspoon of sugar to the blender.
- Blend the mixture until smooth
- If it is very runny, add some cornstarch to make it more viscous.
- Transfer it to the moss paint container.
- Find a wall where you can apply the moss paint. The wall should have some sunlight reaching it, but should not be in the direct path of the sun all day long. A moister environment is best.
- Apply the paint with the brush on the wall, painting whatever design you like.
- Once you have painted your moss art, refrigerate the remaining mixture.
- Return every 2 days to spray it with a water bottle, and add more paint every other day as well. This is to encourage growth and thriving of the moss painting. It may grow very quickly, or it may grow

a bit slower, depending on the environment.

- To remove the moss graffiti, it must be sprayed with limejuice.

What you should learn:

- Moss is also a photosynthesizing plant! This fun activity demonstrates the amazing ability for plants to grow under all kinds of conditions, and allows students to craft a fun and beautiful living mural.

Questions:

- Did your moss mural grow?
- If not, why do you think this was?
- What kind of environment does moss like? Was there too much or not enough light? Was it too dry?

5. Plant a seed of your choice and grow a plant for your desk at home

What you need:

- A pot
- Potting soil
- A seed of your choice
- Fertilizer of your choice
- Water

What you do:

- This experiment is simple. Plant and grow your seed.

- Do research to find out exactly how much water your plant needs, or what the best kind of fertilizer to use is.

What you should learn:

- This activity is one of reflection and giving back. Plants are the basis for all life here on earth. They allow us to live, and so it is nice to give something back, and to help one grow. After all the amazing things we learned about plants, don't you want one anyway?! You should cultivate this plant, take care of it, and enjoy having another living thing to share your space with.

Questions:

- What did you learn about plants and photosynthesis that was most fascinating for you?
- What kind of plant did you choose to grow?

Weather: Activities and Experiments

1. Investigating evaporation and condensation

What you need:

- Large plastic bowl
- A pitcher
- Ceramic coffee cup
- Large rubber band, or long piece of string
- Water
- Sheet of clear plastic wrap
- Pencil and lab book
- Small rock

What you do:

- Pour water into the bowl until it is about a quarter full.
- Place the coffee cup in the center of the bowl, and make sure there is no water inside.
- Cover the top of the bowl tightly with plastic wrap.
- Secure the wrap in place using the large plastic band or the long string.
- Place the small rock on the plastic wrap in the center, above the cup.

- Make sure the rock is large enough to cause a droop in the plastic wrap, but not large enough to drag it down completely.
- Place the bowl in a sunny warm place.
- Observe and record.

What you should learn:
- The water will evaporate due to the heat, and it will become mist. This mist will condense on the top of the plastic, and drip down into the mug. This is a simulation of the water cycle! Imagine that the water contained in the bowl is like the ocean, the condensation on plastic is like the clouds, and the dripping is like the rain.

Questions:
- What if the water was dirty?
- Would the water that drips in the mug after condensation also be dirty?
- Why or why not? If you are not sure, just give it a try!

2. Creating a tornado in a bottle
What you need:
- 2 1 liter plastic bottles
- Water
- Bowl
- Strong, duct tape
- Metal washer that fits on top of the mouth of a bottle

What you do:
- Remove the labels from the bottles and clean them.
- Fill 1 bottle to the top, and put the metal washer on the opening.
- Place the second, empty water bottle on top of the first one, so that the washer sits between them.
- Use the duct tape to secure the two bottles together. Make this connection very strong by tightly applying several layers of tape. No movement should occur.
- Turn the device over and swirl the water as it drains. The water will form a tornado as it drains into the second bottle!

What you should learn:
- This fun simulation of a tornado shows us how the vortex shape forms. The vortex is the shape that occurs in liquids and gasses that causes them to spin in spirals around a central point, as it does in a tornado.

Question:
- In what kind of conditions do tornados arise?
- Which parts of the world (and of your country, if applicable) are the most susceptible to tornados? You may need to research this question.

3. Simulating the greenhouse effect

What you need:
- 2 thermometers
- 2 small glass jars
- 2 liter soda bottle
- Scissors
- Pencil and lab book

What you do:
- Place the 2 thermometers in the small glass jars, and place the 2 glass jars in a sunny place.
- Using the scissors, remove the label and cut the top half of the bottle off.
- Keeping the cap on, use the top half of the bottle to cover one of the jars with its thermometer.
- Wait 1 hour.
- Observe and record the temperature from both thermometers.

What you should learn:
- The thermometer inside of the bottle should display a higher temperature. This is due to the greenhouse effect. The solar energy that passes into the contained area of the bottle half is turned into heat energy, which is trapped inside the bottle. The earth also has its own kind of 'bottle'. This bottle is the atmosphere. This is how our earth retains heat.

Question:

- Why is it important for us, as humans, to not alter the makeup of our atmosphere too much? This is a very broad question, and requires some research to answer. Do some research on greenhouse gasses and global warming to find out the answer!

4. Heat convection in liquid

What you need:
- Clear jar
- Water
- Freezer
- Spoon
- Liquid dropper
- Coffee cup
- Food coloring

What you do:
- Fill the jar three quarters with cold water, and put it in the freezer to cool even further. The water should become cold, but not freeze.
- Full the coffee mug half way with hot water.
- Add food-coloring drops until water is a strong shade of blue.
- Remove jar with cold water and put it on the bench.
- Fill the dropper with hot blue water, and lower the dropper to the bottom of the jar. Release a few drops of blue water and observe what happens.

- Record your results.
- Add more blue water, and observe what happens.
- Once you have added some blue water with dropper, wait 5 more minutes and observe what happens.
- Record your results.

What you should learn:
- When you squeeze the hot water drops out, they rise to the top. Because they are hotter and contain more kinetic energy, the molecules are moving around more and more, making the hot water less dense than the cold water. This causes it to rise. Over time, the temperatures equalize, and the blue liquid diffuses throughout the entire jar.

Question:
- What parallels can you draw between this experiment and what we learned in the unit?

5. Creating a weather chart an compare to predictions

What you need:
- Your pencil and lab book
- A computer with internet
- A thermometer
- A camera and printer (optional)

What you do:

- Go online and search for the weather for the next week in your city or place of residence.
- Draw a chart in your lab book, labeling the upcoming 7 days, and the expected weather forecast for those days.
- Each day go outside and assess the weather. Leave a thermometer somewhere outside and look at it once in the morning, once in the afternoon, and once in the evening.
- Use these measurements to give an average temperature for the day.
- Take photos of any clouds, and print them and include them in your lab book.
- Identify which cloud type they may be, and label them.
- Compare the weather forecast with the actual weather, and assess whether the forecast was accurate or not.

What you should learn:
- Forecasting the weather is not an easy job! Sometimes the forecast is correct, and sometimes it is flawed. Because of the great complexity of the task, and the great many number of variables involved, we are not yet perfect predictors of the weather, but still manage to do a pretty good job.

Questions:
- Was the weather forecast accurate or not?

- How do meteorologists forecast the weather in the first place?

Made in the USA
Lexington, KY
13 February 2018